Grantham
in Focus

Volume 2

GRANTHAM
Journal

at heart ♡ publications

With special thanks to the following readers:

Chris & Bette Davis
Paul Hadlow
Arthur Hides
Paul Johnson
Maureen Wendy Money
Gordon & Veronica Reedman
Kathy, John & William Rose
Peter Straker
Alan Tabiner

First published in 2008 by
At Heart Ltd
32 Stamford Street
Altrincham
Cheshire
WA14 1EY

in conjunction with
The Grantham Journal
46 High Street
Grantham
NG31 6NE

Images: © 2008 Grantham Journal
Text: © 2008 John Pinchbeck

ISBN: 978-1-84547-209-2

Printed and bound by Ashford Colour Press, Gosport.

Contents

JOHN PINCHBECK was born in Grantham to a family long associated with the town. On his father's side, he can trace his ancestry to 1690, when the family was already settled in Grantham.

The author has worked for several county newspapers, including the *Grantham Journal*, *Lincolnshire Echo* and *Sleaford Standard*. He retired from the *Journal* in 2007.

The series *Grantham in the News* was conceived in the archives of the *Grantham Journal*, where he spent many of his lunch hours, poring over old newspapers to retrieve long-forgotten stories.

A pupil at St Anne's School, Dudley Road, and later the Boys' Central, Sandon Road, he has seen many changes in the town both good and bad and still gets a thrill of wandering down places such as Vere Court, Inner Street and Spring Gardens, just to reflect on how unromantic life was for the poor wretches who lived or worked there.

He has published a number of titles on Grantham which cover over a century of the town's history.

ACKNOWLEDGEMENTS

THIS book is dedicated to the *Journal* photographers who recorded the town over the years including: Ron Dean, Peter Dean, Vic Pell, Max Ewen, Gerry Wright, Jeff Carter and Toby Roberts.

Also thanks to readers who allowed me to use their pictures, including: Helen Ash, Kathleen Aspland, Sheila Bailey, Peter Ball, Chris Bennett, Charles Bolland, C R Braisby, John Brammer, Derrick Clarke, Barrie Cox, Ron Crowson, Vince Eager, George Emery, Dave Fardell, Peter Gaskell, Ian Graves, Keith Harrison, Josie Hemstock, Bunty Heppenstall, Shirley Hind, Malcolm G. Knapp, Pam Lea-Hair, David Maltby, Stan Matthews, Mike Matsell, Arthur McKown, Dave Morgan, Kate Morgan, Susan Morgan, Peter Nicholls, Sheila Osborn, Joan Parnham, Paddy Perry, Sue Redmile, Peter Reichelt, Terry Shelbourne, Ron Slater, Ken Snell, Neville Spick, Hazel Tebb, Harry Thomas, Jeff Thompson, Joyce Tilley, Audrey Vaughan, Clarry Vickers, Sheila Ward, Gladys Watchorn and Patricia Wolfenden.

Introduction

IN this, the second book of the series, we have unearthed many more old and new pictures, many never before published.

Many have been loaned to me by *Grantham Journal* readers, which complement those taken by the newspaper's staff photographers.

Among the features are pictures from the workplace. These include TDG, Wolsey and Caddy Castings.

There are some excellent photographs in the winter wonderland section and some fascinating pictures taking during the Second World War.

Another new section takes a look at celebrity visits through the years, featuring stars and politicians mingling with locals.

We have also unearthed some very interesting pictures of village life as well as pictures of schooldays. This is on top of town pictures, not only focusing on the popular parts of town, but some rare pictures of Union Street and Harrow Street.

Anyone with unusual pictures of Grantham or the surrounding area, who would like them published in a subsequent volume, can contact me through the Grantham Journal or email granthampast@gmail.com.

I hope the reader will enjoy browsing this book as much as I enjoyed compiling it.

John R. Pinchbeck, July 2008

London Road and South Parade

LONDON Road has changed as much as any in the town, with only a few buildings to the north surviving modern developments. Even the sports ground disappeared when the cricket club moved to Gorse Lane and the footballers relocated to Trent Road.

■ CHILDREN today would not be strolling across the road at the St Peter's Hill junction with London Road as they did in 1904.

■ ONE of the oldest pictures in this book, of the original Nag's Head pub on the corner of Wharf Road in 1883. Part of Spittlegate House can be seen to the left. The building was about to be demolished, to be replaced by a more substantial public house.

■ LONDON Road looking north in 1908. Apart from the trees, it has changed little in more than a century.

■ THE St Peter's Hill end of London Road in 1980. The old lock-up shops are now gone, replaced by Leonard Audus House, and the Nag's Head has become a restaurant.

■ THE buildings may be the same, but the businesses have long gone. Motor engineers Speediweld moved to Dysart Road, and the mock-Tudor building was taken over by Just Tyres which closed in 2000 following a major fire.

■ SOME of the 6,000 spectators queuing outside the football ground for Grantham FC's FA Cup second preliminary round tie against Boston United in 1954.

   The Blue Horse was still a pub, although it was later converted to a fish and chip shop. There are some classic 1950s vehicles in the car park pictured here.

■ MORE spectators turn out for Grantham's 1954 FA Cup round against Boston United. The background shows Ruston and Hornsby's London Road factory to the right.

■ GRANTHAM Motor Company's art deco-style building in 1990, about nine years before the bulldozers moved in. The clock, which had been a timepiece for workers going to Ruston and Hornsby and Aveling Barford, was electric-powered by a clockwork generator. Unfortunately it wasn't saved during the demolition.

■ THE old Grantham Motor Company premises being demolished in 1999 to make way for a new retail park.

■ A FORD lorry in the Grantham Motor Company showroom in 1955. Outside, a car is filling up at the petrol pumps.

■ THE parts department at Grantham Motors in 1955, long before computers were introduced.

■ TAKEN in 1980, these shops were on London Road. Hairloom was housed in the Masonic Hall, built on a former builders' yard in 1907, to replace the one on St Peter's Hill. The Freemasons later moved to Chambers Street.

■ THE old Ruston & Hornsby factory in 1988. The top floor of the building on the right once housed the rifle range for the company's rifle club. It was demolished to make way for Halfords. The people, incidentally, are waiting for the Grantham Carnival parade.

■ SOUTH Parade looked almost rural when this picture was taken in 1912. The houses on the left are still there, while the trees on the right disguise the heavy industrial factories of the time.

St Peter's Hill

ALWAYS changing yet ever recognisable, the centre of Grantham and the hub of South Kesteven is the administrative area of town, with both council offices, three banks and the main post office.

■ ST Peter's Hill in 1901 was a quiet place. The tall building on the right became the public library for a short spell, before being demolished for a purpose-built one on the same site.

■ A PARADE marches along St Peter's Hill in 1946. This picture, taken from the air, gives a rare view of the area. On the left is the old post office, with two former town houses converted into shops next door.

■ AN unusual view of the Guildhall taken from the air in 1946. Look carefully and you can still see the blast wall in front to protect it from bombs. Outbuildings on the left include the police station (with a flat roof) and the fire station, which moved to Harlaxton Road a couple of years later. Also pictured is the bus station waiting room.

■ THE building known as the Birdcage is still there today, but looks less impressive since much of the ironwork was removed. The building next to it was demolished to make way for the Job Centre.

■ WHEN this picture was taken in 1948, the St Peter's Hill junction linked five roads, the one on the right serving a busy bus station. The concrete lampposts were quite new, having been erected by Italian prisoners of war.

■ THE General Post Office in 1960. It was built in the 1920s when the post office moved from Market Place, and was demolished about 12 years after this picture was taken, to be replaced by a modern one.

■ A VERY peaceful scene on St Peter's Hill in 1960. Through the trees you can see the old post office. The three shops are Sterne Austin (greengrocer) Maison Meta (milliners) and Clarks of Retford (laundry).

■ THE Granada Bingo Hall in 1980. Built as the 1,400-seat State cinema in 1937, it was relegated to a bingo hall after the final film, *Tales of Beatrix Potter*, was shown in 1972.

■ HEALTH workers demonstrating on St Peter's Hill in 1988. The green has always been a central point for rallies.

■ THIS 19th century photograph of the former Chief Constable and Inspector of Weights and Measures' house was taken in the Guildhall Yard.

High Street, Watergate, North Street and North Parade

HIGH Street and Watergate saw some fine buildings demolished after the Second World War, only to be replaced by less substantial modern ones.

■ WATERGATE in 1936, looking towards the town centre. The tall building on the right is Harrison's.

■ THIS 1920 picture captures High Street starting to come to terms with the 20th century. On the left is the Georgian inn, The George Hotel, with its archway for stagecoaches. Across the road is Whipples Garage for the modern motorist. The ivy-covered building on the right is the Midland Bank, which was demolished 13 years later to make way for Marks & Spencer. The building in the background, later to become Newton Fallowell estate agents, was National Provincial Bank.

■ HIGH Street looking north in 1916, where the only serious traffic problem is a handcart. The George Hotel is on the left.

■ THIS Tudor window was in the yard at the rear of Catlin's shop and cafe. It was removed when Marks & Spencer built a new store in 1933 and bought by the Misses Sedgwick for Grantham House. Most of the other stone features were used as hardcore for the new building.

■ THE rear of the *Journal* before demolition in 1957, when the new building, incorporating F.W. Woolworth at the front, was built.

■ FOR many years this corner shop was Knightingale's stationers, but Harrison's had moved along High Street from opposite Woolworth's before this picture was taken in 1970. Next door is Beevers, the town's last drapers.

■ THESE buildings, pictured in 1978, are still there today, but the businesses have moved. The building to the left was the National Westminster Bank (formerly National Provincial and later NatWest), H. H. Cox moved to Westgate and Burtons moved next door to Marks & Spencer.

■ HARRISON'S shop, Watergate, decorated to celebrate Queen Victoria's Diamond Jubilee 1897. The company sold prams, travel goods and osier products. It had an osier works in Westbourne Place, off Dysart Road, and behind this shop.

■ TELEPHONE engineers, carrying a telegraph pole from Leicester to Skegness, passed through town on their way in 1981. They were raising funds for the maternity unit at Leicester Royal Infirmary. They are seen here passing along Watergate.

■ Passing through Market Place.

■ NEVER ones to miss out on a party, the people of Grantham decorate in style for Queen Victoria's Golden Jubilee in 1887. Dawson's (later Sharpley's) was demolished in the 1950s to widen Watergate.

■ THE old pie shop on the corner of North Street and Union Street. Situated next door to Leyland motor dealership R.M. Wright in the 1970s, it still bore the address 'Blue Lion Lane'.

■ WATERGATE, looking towards North Street, in 1910.

■ COLLARDS had already closed the Little Dustpan, in Westgate, when this picture of the Watergate shop was taken in 1978. The shop sold everything from shotguns to general ironmongery. Next door is Vauxhall dealership, Whipples.

■ THE Watergate surgery, and home of Dr Peter Shipman. He closed the surgery when he moved to work full-time at Grantham Hospital. The building was demolished as part of the Watergate road widening scheme in the 1960s.

■ DEMOLITION continues on Watergate in 1964, and billboards at the foot of the hill disguise even more bulldozing. On the left is Paints, John Coxworth's decorating and artists' shop, while behind is the gable of the four-storey Harrison's building, which also had a limited future.

■ WATERGATE House in 1977, showing the Toy Cabin and Granada TV Rental at a time when it was usual to rent televisions rather than purchase them.

■ SWEET shop and tobacconist Welbourn and Son was the last shop on the east side of North Street, before the last blow from the bulldozers in the 1980s. Vere Street and James Street had already come down for what eventually became Premier Court.

■ THE Post Office on the corner of North Parade and Broad Street became iconic in the 1980s as the birthplace of Prime Minister Margaret Thatcher. This photograph was taken in the early 1900s, when the site was owned by Parkers. Mrs Thatcher's father, Alfred Roberts, bought it from them.

Wharf Road to Launder Terrace

WHARF Road has seen some dramatic changes since 1980, although the streets to the south have seen more gentle alterations.

■ SAMUEL Willows and his wife, grocery and provision dealers, outside their shop at 63 Brewery Hill, Spittlegate, in about 1900.

■ JIM Baxter's Victorian Bazaar in 1982 was housed in the former Hand and Heart pub. Jim, one of the town's great characters, had a house-clearing business selling furniture and knick-knacks from this shop. Next door was a knitwear shop.

■ WHEN Rutland Street was demolished in 1981, this digger driver overturned his machine after it collapsed into a cellar, nearly knocking down the maltings as well. Fortunately, no-one was hurt.

■ THE slipper baths, Wharf Road, in 1982. These were not for swimming, but for taking a bath in a time when fewer people had their own bathrooms. This building, on the corner of Bath Street, was demolished shortly after this picture was taken.

■ THE Maltings were hidden for many years until Jackson Bros garage was demolished in the early 1980s to build Wharf Road roundabout. They were later restored as offices.

■ SOME of
the businesses
on the south
side of Wharf
Road in 1983.

■ SHOPS along Wharf Road awaiting demolition in 1983. The wool shop on the left was still open, but chemists, John Cheshire, was closed and the businesses in the former Durham Ox pub were preparing to shut.

■ THE Big Top came to town in April 1961, and elephants marched from the railway station to the circus in Wyndham Park. Crowds turned out to watch them as they set off down Station Road (West). In the background is Coultas's woodyard.

■ JACKSON Shipley's Grantham depot in Commercial Road during the 1970s. It later moved to the former Ruston and Hornsby 'Top End', South Parade and became Jackson Building Supplies.

■ RAILWAY Terrace in 1984 looking towards Norton Street, when the building on the left, formerly the Three Tuns pub, was a second-hand bookshop.

■ A FORMER shop in Norton Street. More than 180 people signed a petition in 1980 when it was earmarked as a home for mentally ill people. The street seems less cluttered with cars than of late.

■ ST John's Hall was in Launder Terrace. It was pulled down a few years ago and replaced by flats. Originally a town house, it was built by the Coultas family who ran an engineering works (and later a woodyard) in town. In the 1930s it was taken over by St John's Church and an extension built for meetings. It was requisitioned by the military during the war and used mainly for medicals for both recruits and conscientious objectors, then as a warehouse for Grantham Co-Operative Society. Despite its condition externally, it was used as a dance studio until just before its demolition.

■ THIS pair of houses in Launder Terrace have enjoyed a varied history, although the two-storey homes next door were demolished to make way for council flats in Commercial Road.

From 1844 to 1884, the pair were home to Spittlegate (later Spitalgate) School, until a bigger school was built across the road. In the 1980s, the house to the right became a joke shop. The house to the left was Hill's shop in the 1970s and previously Parnham's.

Westgate and Market Place

BOTH Westgate and Market Place remained relatively unchanged as the rest of the town developed. Naturally, shop frontages changed over the years but generally most buildings managed to survive.

■ THE Bridge Inn, Westgate, close to Harlaxton Road railway bridge, in 1977. It was knocked down to widen the road for a roundabout.

■ D.E. CHANDLER'S shop in 1951. The doorway was soon to be filled in to improve the windows. The company claimed it could supply everything from a cotter pin to a combine harvester.

■ INSIDE D.E. Chandler's shop in 1960.

■ WIDE Westgate was a very muddy road when this picture was taken in 1897. The coach was taking clients from the railway station to the Angel and Royal Hotel.

■ TAKEN in 1978, The Gun Shop appears to be in a time warp. Thirty years later, very little has changed.

■ ONLY A limited number of local businesses survived the 1980s, but at least three of the shops on this picture are still going strong. The popular Record Shop has gone, but is part of Watkins expansion. Angelo's fish and chip shop and newsagents, and Arthur Creese are also still there at the time of going to press.

■ FOSTERS newsagents and post office in Westgate, taken in about 1980. The building was in the way of The George development, but the pillar box remained.

■ JOHN Barber's decorating shop in about 1980, next door to Sharpe's seed shop.

■ THE Little Dustpan, the symbol of Collards the ironmongers, remained after the company had closed its doors and become Stan Horsley's toy and cycle shop. Cameo Cameras and the Flower Shop were also there in 1985.

■ EARLY work on The George Centre as Grantham Book Centre, Westgate, gets attention in 1990.

■ THIS odd view of Westgate is one seldom seen. It is the roof of Club iT, the former Westgate Hall.

■ THIS picture, taken along Westgate in 2007, shows just how much the Harlaxton Road maltings dominate the town.

■ A LARGE crowd assembled around the market cross in 1911 to hear the proclamation of King George V as the new monarch.

■ THE snack bar in Market Place has always been popular, as this picture from the 1970s shows.

■ THE *Grantham Shopper*, a free newspaper started in 1975, was part of an estate agent's. The office in Butchers Row – once Ellis's, Grantham's first milk bar – was closed when the *Shopper* moved to Watergate House. It left in 1985, as part of the *Journal*.

■ ONLY Skinner's remained 28 years after this 1980 picture was taken in a part of Market Place once known as Coal Hill. Burton moved across High Street, and Watkin's concentrated on its Westgate branch.

■ LADIES' shop Hill and Co had closed when this picture was taken in 1985.

■ MARKET Place in 1985, with Jonathan James' shoe shop and Paddy McBride's fish and chip shop. Oxfam was also established here around this time.

■ MARKET Place in 1985. Like so many pictures from this era, little has changed but for the name over the door.

■ ELIZABETH Charles, Fine Furnishings, Mark Jarvis turf accountants and Notions antiques in Market Place in 1990.

■ MARKET Place in 1885. There was only a narrow entrance into Conduit Lane until the Blue Sheep was demolished. The picture also shows the Blue Lion and the Granby. Clearly there was no lack of places to drink in those days!

■ A CRYPT was discovered under a building in Butchers Row on 26 April 1888. Unfortunately, this fine example of medieval craftsmanship was not preserved.

■ OWNED by Buckminster Trust and rented to a photographic company, this building was almost unknown, until it was gutted by a blaze in 2001. It was situated behind Notions Antiques in Market Place. You can just see Westgate Hall (later Jaspers and Club iT) across the road.

Guildhall Street

OVER the years, Guildhall Street has altered more than any other in town. In 1860, it was home to the Guildhall, and the town jail. Even since 1989 it has changed enormously.

■ THE roof over The George Centre, Guildhall Street.

■ GUILDHALL Street in 1977 was very different to today. These stone buildings were knocked down to make way for The George Centre.

■ GUILDHALL Street in 1978 with few changes other than being a little tidier.

■ THE former George Tap, Guildhall Street, before it was demolished to make way for The George shopping centre in 1989.

■ ANOTHER view of the George Tap, showing the courtyard of the George Hotel.

■ THE Guildhall Street side of Waterloo House in 1985, before it was pulled down to make way for a new block of shops.

■ WATERLOO House on the corner of Guildhall Street and High Street.

■ THE rear of Waterloo House, High Street, as seen from The George Hotel car park, Guildhall Street, in 1985.

■ THE rear of the George Hotel, taken in 1989, shortly before its closure for development.

■ MOTOR dealer Campion Depot was on the south side of Guildhall Street, a site later occupied by Argos. It sold Rootes Group cars, which included marques Hillman, Humber and Sunbeam.

The showroom moved in the late 1960s to the corner of London Road and Spring Gardens, a site once occupied by Ruston and Hornsby's foundry. The picture shows local rock 'n' roll star Vince Eager taking delivery of a Humber Sceptre.

■ TAKEN in June 1990, this shows St Peter's Place (later The George) shopping centre being built around the George Hotel. The wing to the left was the ground floor ballroom.

Little Gonerby and Gonerby Hill Foot

UNTIL 1978, the town north of Brook Street was a separate parish called Little Gonerby. Like Spittlegate, Earlesfield, New Somerby, Houghton and Walton, and Harrowby Within, it became part of the enlarged Grantham.

■ CHILDREN and parents in the rather inaccurately named Paradise Place, off New Street. They were celebrating Grantham Civic Week in 1935.

■ CALIFORNIA Gardens were a well-kept secret until the owner decided to sell the land at the end of Maltings Lane, Gonerby Hill Foot, to developers in 2007. These allotment holders are protesting at losing their land after years of uninterrupted use. Barrowby Road estate in the background is an indication of what was in store.

■ VERE Court, which ran off Broad Street between New Street and North Parade, being demolished in the 1930s. The living conditions in these homes were appalling.

Signs on the float read:

SUGAR BEET THE ROOT TO PROSPERITY

SUGAR BEET IS THE KEYSTONE of FARMING SEE IT CONTINUES

■ WITH the horse is Walter Culpin, of Marston, with his corporation farm float on his way to the Silver Jubilee celebrations of King George V in Grantham. The ladies are Mrs Ivy Bartholomew and Mrs Vera Clarke. They are waiting outside the cottage in Gonerby Hill Foot, not far from the Lord Nelson pub.

■ INSIDE St Saviour's Church, Manners Street, at the turn of the 20th century.

Around town

THIS section is about the smaller streets and lesser-photographed areas near the town centre that even locals might have missed.

■ CHILDREN enjoying themselves in the Harrow Street back yards in 1905.

■ AVENUE Road at the Grove End Road junction in the 1900s. It hardly changed for nearly a century, until the building on the right (the county court) was demolished.

■ DEMOLITION of the former county court, Grove End Road, in 1999. The building was declared unsafe.

■ TAKEN in about 1960, this old house stood at the top of Avenue Road, and was the Grantham Borough Council-owned rates office. It was knocked down and replaced by the flat-roofed building at the end of Abbey Gardens.

■ A CREW negotiates its way under Stonebridge in September 1982, in the annual raft races. Unfortunately, the event later fell foul of hefty insurance premiums. And while Stonebridge Road still runs over it, the bridge is no longer stone, having been replaced by metal railings in about 2000.

■ THESE remains were said to be of a Franciscan Priory that stood in a garden off Union Street, in the 17th century. In fact, they are a garden folly designed by the then Priory owner and businessman Arthur Chambers. He called it St Egelwyne's Priory.

These are the ruins as seen in about 1900, although they are still there and were often used by wedding photographers up to about 2007, when the Register Office moved from the Priory to Springfield House.

■ THIS historic picture from 1935 was taken in Union Street. It shows neighbours outside their homes decorated for Civic Week, in June, to celebrate a century of Grantham Borough Council. The borough coat of arms is over the home of the chimney sweep, who has built an aeroplane with the caption "Chimney sweep 100 years from now". The houses stood roughly on the site of Hunters Bar. The fence to the right is Harrison's osier factory.

■ THESE two large houses in Union Street are now under the Asda car park. They were pulled down to make way for an indoor swimming pool, and were roughly behind Leyland dealer R.M. Wright's workshop. The one on the right was once owned by scrap merchant Charles Spick, whose business was in Union Street.

■ THE old building is Dudley House, Dudley Road, which was demolished in about 1969 to make way for Dudley House School. Taken in 1901, it shows the family of William Lee, son of John Lee, who had given his name to a generation of local companies and was a pioneer in recycling. Many locals will remember John Lee's factory along Hands Yard, running alongside the Granada cinema, where rabbit pellets were hung to dry.

The picture shows William and his wife Mary (seated left) with family and friends. It includes their children Rothwell (who became Mayor of Grantham), Grace, Marion, Elizabeth, Carlton, Godfrey, Holdsworth, Silverwood and Hatfield.

■ OUTDOOR privies in Old Wharf Cottages, Old Wharf Road.

■ A SWEET shop owned by John Henry Saville, 11 Vine Street, in 1937.

■ YOUNGSTERS were joined by councillors on a march through town in 1961. They were protesting at the George Hotel management's decision to try to get rock 'n' roll dances banned at the Westgate Hall. Four hundred led a silent protest. The procession is seen in Elmer Street South, where many of the buildings have since been demolished.

■ THE rear of High Street shoe shop, J. Porter and Son, in Elmer Street South. The business began in the 19th century in Elmer Street, and only closed in the 1980s.

■ THE old Mission in Eton Street was a car repair workshop in 1982. The interior was badly damaged by fire the following year.

■ A VIEW from Grantham College in 1982. The main building, set apart from St Wulfram's, is Crown House. Since then, Riverside complex has been built.

■ HOUSES in Harlaxton Road were in the firing line of a gale that swept through the town in January 1976. Builders were soon on the scene carrying out repairs.

■ THE Crown and Anchor, Swinegate, shortly after it closed in 1936.

■ TWO shops on Dudley Road in the 1960s. Nearest to the camera is Lou Mapletoft's barber's shop. His window always boasted a display of Brylcream, in all its various forms! Next door is newsagents Hatton and Matchett. The first partner was Cyril Hatton, a local boy who played for Queen's Park Rangers and Notts County before returning to manage his home town club.

■ THE former Crown and Anchor, Swinegate, in 1983, when it was a parts depot for motor dealership R.M. Wright.

■ GILBERTS health food shop, showing the former Crown and Anchor in the background.

■ ONCE the Rose and Crown pub had been pulled down in about 1985 to make way for a nursing home, the rears of these Georgian properties in Church Trees were exposed.

■ AN old Grantham business, greengrocer Arnold Graham, in Swinegate.

■ AT one time, this was one of Grantham's oldest motor dealers, G.R. Burton, who specialised in Morris cars. It was later taken over by Temple Saunders, but the building has had a number of occupants since, from data processors to beauticians.

■ FORMERLY the Zion Independent Church, this building in Castlegate has had many uses in recent years, including a pine centre (as here) in 1985, a gymnasium and a children's nursery.

■ THE Beehive, Castlegate, has a unique 'living' inn sign... a real hive, full of bees!

■ BLUEGATE in the 1960s. The stone wall and houses on the left were knocked down to make way for alms houses some 20 years later.

Out of town

AWAY from the centre of town, there is still plenty of interest going on in Grantham.

■ RESIDENTS of Brittain Drive and Range Road holding one of many street parties in town to celebrate the wedding of Prince Charles and Lady Diana Spencer in July 1981. To be the first of the bunch, these residents held their party five days before the royal event!

■ THE poplar trees on
Barrowby Road in 1953

■ PRINCESS Drive was
formally opened by the Mayor
of Grantham, Ernest Hardy,
in 1954. Next to him is
Alderman Jenkinson,
chairman of West Kesteven
Rural Council.

The road was planned to be
the first part of a ring road for
Grantham.

■ GRANTHAM from the hills to the south of the town in 2007, showing the new Springfield Park estate in the foreground and Earlesfield in the background.

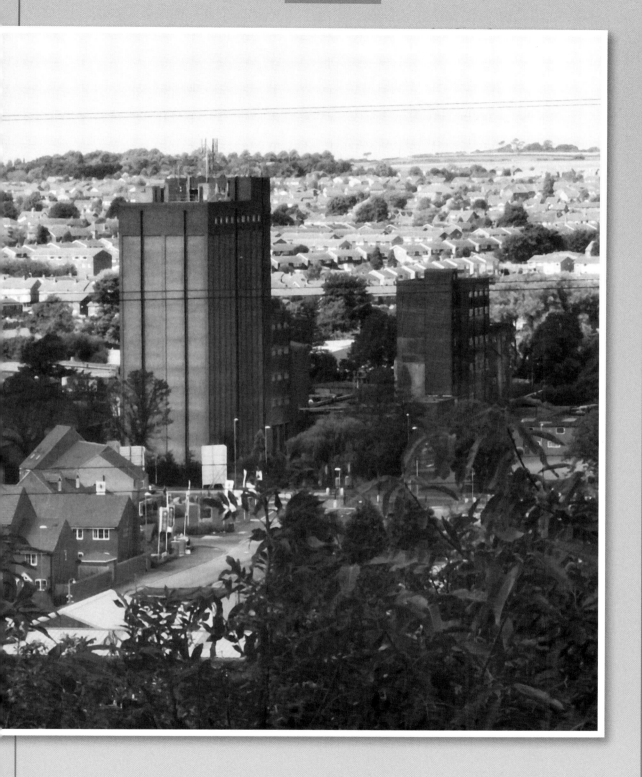

■ NEW homes being built at the junction of Stamford Street and Springfield Road in 1977. It was built on the site of Springfield Mission. Through the poplar trees, the former Ruston and Hornsby's South Parade works are visible. By then, they were being used as a spares department by Aveling Barford.

■ AIRE Road flats were about to get a £75,000 facelift when this photograph was taken in 1985. Built in 1961, the five blocks of 12 flats were often the target of vandals. They were also unpopular with tenants, with communal clothes drying and refuse facilities far away from the properties.

■ AIRE Road flats being demolished in 2004.

■ RESIDENTS of Ninth Avenue were never ones to turn down the chance to party. They are pictured here in May 1985 celebrating the 40th anniversary of VE Day.

■ B&B Garages, Spittlegate Level, in 1990. It was later to become the site of Grantham Motor Company, and then Evans Halshaw.

■ THE Inner Relief Road – later to be called Sankt Augustin Way – at the Westgate end. The road was originally to run along Station Road (West) and continue to Gainsborough Corner. This was scotched, however, when the rail companies did an about turn and refused the use of their property.

■ ENTERPRISING schoolboys in Walton Gardens created their own skate park in 2001. Rather than wait for the council to build one in Wyndham Park, Damon McAndrew, Daniel Herbert, Perry Smith, Jack Whyley and Karl Spain built a ramp and half-pipe outside some lock-up garages.

■ WARMINGTON Hall, Derwent Road, which had in its time been a women's refuge and a hostel for young footballers signed by Grantham Town FC, was sold for £150,000 to be converted into flats in 2001. However, the plans were never fulfilled. When a blaze destroyed the property it was demolished and the site redeveloped.

■ WARMINGTON Hall following the fire in October 2004.

Villages

GRANTHAM is surrounded by some of the most beautiful and fascinating villages in the country.

■ FOSTON Long Street pictured in about 1905.

■ FARMERS congregate at Fulbeck Airfield in May 1986 before setting off on a rolling road block to Grantham. They were part of the LAND (Lincolnshire Against Nuclear Dumping) campaign objecting to Government agency Nirex's plans to landfill low-level radioactive waste.

■ CAYTHORPE railway station at the beginning of the 20th century, where there was no shortage of manpower.

■ WORK on the £10,000 Caythorpe bypass came to a halt when two women refused to leave their home, which was in the way. Mary Anne Scott (87) and her daughter Elsie May (60) lived in the house that prevented contractors from linking it up with the Grantham–Lincoln road, leaving the bypass just 40 metres short. They had been offered a council house but Miss Scott said: "Why should we pay an extortionate rent out of our pensions? We intend to remain until a suitable offer is made, even if it means staying here while they demolish our home around us."

■ FOSTON Dovecote in around 1910. Built in medieval times, it was made of mud, bonded with straw and pebbles. It was bulldozed in 1960 to make way for the A1 Foston bypass.

■ FOSTON Main Street in the 1930s.

■ LONG BENNINGTON in 1930, when the Maypole was a popular feature on May Day.

The picture was taken in Winters Lane. The two boys on bicycles are Tom Tebb and Arthur Southern.

■ LOCK HOUSE, by the side of the Grantham Canal in Stenwith, had no water, no electricity and no sewerage system, when this picture was taken in 1933. Jack and Margaret Topps lived in the tied cottage during the 1930s where Jack was a lengthsman, responsible for keeping the waterway and towpaths clear between Woolsthorpe and Redmile.

Lighting in the house was first by Kelly lamps and later by Tilly lamps, both fuelled by paraffin. The water came through filter-beds in the ground, which were cleaned out every year, and the toilet was a bucket in a small building away from the house which was emptied daily and dug into the garden.

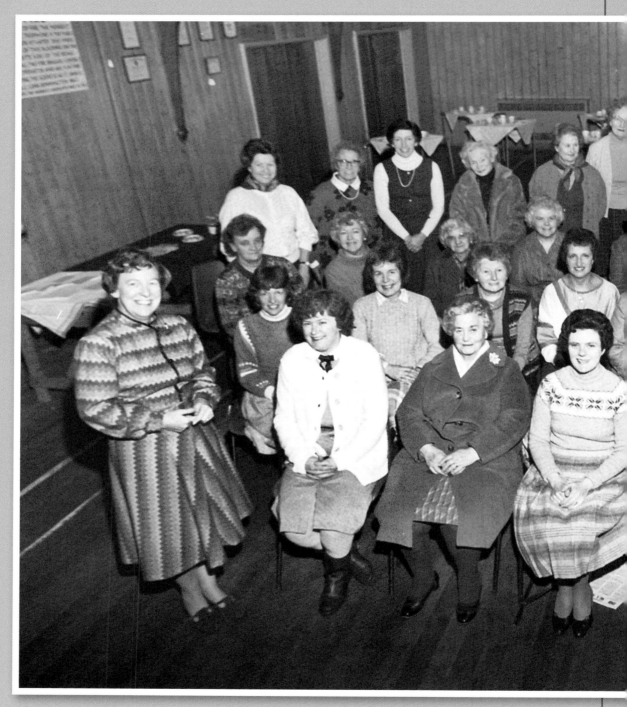

■ LONG BENNINGTON Women's Institute inside the old village hall in 1985. The branch was formed in 1918, with Mrs Younghusband as its first president. She invested £40 so that members could enjoy a birthday cake every year. To celebrate the diamond jubilee in 1978, they planted a maple tree on the village green and, in 1984, members planted 1,000 crocuses on the green.

■ FOLKINGHAM became one of the first villages in south Lincolnshire to make a special effort towards the Festival of Britain in June 1951. Unfortunately, the day began with drizzle and ended in torrential rain, although the festivities still managed to raise £118.

The event was held at Woodlands, owned by Mr J. Rose. It began with a fancy dress parade through the village led by the Grantham Salvation Army Band.

They were followed by a horse-drawn vehicle with Festival Queen Jane Smith and her attendants Jean Holmes and Ann Dawson with Festival of Britain (Gillian Foster).

Pictured left are some participants of the fancy dress parade. The winners were Lindsay Harrod (old lady), Alistair Spencer (jockey), Gillian Foster (Festival of Britain), Peter Coleman (strawberry), Carol Rouse (boxer), Betty Towers (Britannia), Susan Stagg (peasant girl), and Neville Chapman (Wee Willy Winkie).

■ MADGE Manton's garden in Folkingham was quite an attraction in 1971. She built a Disneyland-style miniature village in her West Street garden. It was made out of scraps which most people would throw away.

■ BELTON Church in 1953.

■ DENTON. The Rev Victor Daws, Rector of Denton was a smash with the lady tennis players when he umpired a tournament at Denton fete in 1954. He is pictured with the Misses L. Rawding, C. Daws, B. Measures, S. Shipman, W. Scoffield and V. Homer.

■ SCHOOLBOYS enjoy the lucky dip at Denton fête in 1954.

■ TORRENTIAL rain failed to stop the children at Denton School from their May Pole dance at the May Day street market in 1986. And music didn't suffer either. Martin Crush ensured Infants teacher Elizabeth Wilkinson was protected from the elements.

■ BILLINGBOROUGH crossroads on 2 November 1968, when the whole village was under water. The village fire engine is pumping out water from a house.

■ HARLAXTON Manor echoed to the sound of marching feet and motorcycles, during the filming of *The Last Days of General Patton*, for CBNS television, starring George Scott in the title role. He was reprising his part in the 1970 film *Lust for Glory*. Eva Marie Saint played his wife and Richard Dysart was General Eisenhower. Harlaxton Manor was chosen as the setting for the Third Army HQ, Bavaria.

■ PLANS to form an international shooting range in a 42-acre disused quarry owned by Buckminster Trust did not go down well with villagers in 1985. These Sproxton children also objected, including Josephine Smith (12) who wrote to Prime Minister Margaret Thatcher for support.

■ NINETEENTH century transport meets its successor in about 1910 on High Street, Castle Bytham.

PINFOLD Lane, Castle Bytham, at the beginning of the 20th century.

CHORISTERS, led by Alastair Parsons, make their way with the village band through Woolsthorpe-by-Belvoir on Rogation Sunday, 1962, for the ceremony of blessing the crops.

Winter wonderland

WHEN the snow falls, everything looks different. Here are a few shots taken in and around Grantham during the winter months.

■ SCHOOLBOYS enjoy an afternoon in February 1956 on the Grantham Canal. Behind them is the area known as 'The Willows' which were grown as osier beds by W.B. Harrison in Victorian times.

■ SNOW fell on Market Day in January 1996, leading to an early closure.

■ THE Market was closed at the end of January 1996, thanks to a heavy snowstorm.

■ GRANTHAM awoke to a blanket of snow in January 1996. The residents of Huntingtower Road, pictured here, were in for a surprise.

■ SKATING on the Grantham Canal in 1929.

■ SKATING on the Grantham Canal basin in 1929, next to the sidings of the old Ambergate line.

■ THE snow falling on this January evening in 1947 was just a taste of things to come. It became one of the worst winters in living memory. The picture was taken by *Journal* photographer Ron Dean, who had been on a works outing to the Picture House for the retirement of composing room overseer Mr Dickinson.

■ THE snow was deep and crisp and even in Avenue Road (Stonebridge Road) in January 1958. On the left is the police station, on the right is Kesteven and Grantham Girls School, and further down you can just see the entrance to Grantham College for Further Education.

■ THE main footpath through Wyndham Park in 1973.

■ SNOW covered Wyndham Park in 1973.

■ WINTER isn't all about snowballs and pretty scenery. The snow made roads hazardous as this lorry driver discovered at the top of Denton Hill in January 1977.

■ BMARCo's Springfield Road factory following a snowstorm in 1983. The factory has gone, as has the field, to be replaced by a major housing estate.

■ TAKEN in 1985 from Wyville Road, near the A1 Melton Mowbray sliproad, this photograph shows Earlesfield in the background. Kinoulton Court is being built, but there seems to be a big gap in the warehouses and houses to the left. The reason is that the Meres was still a playing field without a stadium and the industrial estate, which now includes Fenland Foods and the Swallow (later Ramada) Hotel, was yet to be built.

Grantham at war

THE most bombed town of its size during the Second World War, Grantham's citizens had to adapt to new skills in defence, both at work and in their spare time.

■ MOTORCYCLE messengers based at BMARCo in 1942.

■ SANDBAGS were piled high outside the Guildhall in 1940. A blast wall was built later.

■ THE old police cells behind the Guildhall, surrounded by sandbags.

■ "PUT that light out!" Women members of the ARP (Air Raid Precautions) in 1941.

■ MEMBERS of BMARCo Home Guard who shot down a Junkers bomber in 1941 which had attacked their Springfield Road factory. The plane crashed at Frampton, near Boston, and the propeller was subsequently presented to the factory. It hung on the wall until the social club was refurbished in the 1970s and the propeller was sold for scrap.

■ BMARCo, Springfield Road, suffered an air raid in 1941, bombing the joiners shop and No.1 factory.

■ BMARCo's air raid in 1941. This is the south end of Nos.3 and 4 factories belonging to the Ministry of Aircraft Production.

■ A FACTORY worker producing shells at BMARCo during the war.

■ THE blast walls between sections were to protect the workers should their factory be bombed during the Second World War. Helmets were hung on them, and failure to wear them could at best lead to disciplinary action, and at worst a much graver result.

This is Grantham Productions, on London Road, which had taken over part of Ruston & Hornsby for the war. It made Oerlikon gun magazines. A high proportion of the workforce were women.

■ THIRTY-TWO people were killed and 41 injured – nearly half of them seriously – in an October 1942 air raid. More than 600 properties were damaged, 20 demolished and 80 needed extensive repairs. More than 500 people were left homeless.

Most of the casualties were in the Stuart Street area, which was hit by two high-explosive bombs. Several houses in Dudley Road were also damaged. An air raid shelter in Stuart Street (pictured) took a direct hit and was demolished together with a score of homes, killing 20 people.

■ HOUSES in Ermine Close, Uplands Drive, took a direct hit from a German bomber in 1942.

■ TOP brass launch Grantham's Wings for Victory Week outside the Guildhall in 1942. Among the civilians are Alfred Roberts and MP Denis Kendall.

■ GRANTHAM'S Wings for Victory Week in 1942 raised more than a quarter of a million pounds to buy bombers.

■ LAND army girls in 1944 at Hawksworth Hall, near Orston. They were stationed at the 'Hawksworth Hostel' from 1943 to 1949.

Focus on work

OVER the last half of the 20th century, employment in Grantham switched from mainly engineering and plant-making to food processing and service industries.

■ INSIDE the gloomy Bjorlow's tanneries in about 1970.

■ THE offices of Bjorlow's tannery. The factory in the background is on the other side of Earlesfield Lane.

■ WORKMEN building Richard Hornsby's extension on Houghton Road in 1911. The building was taken over by Aveling Barford in the mid-1930s.

■ RUSTON and Hornsby's top foundry, Spring Gardens, in 1926. Men working in these terrible conditions were said to age prematurely.

■ RUSTON and Hornsby packing department busy stencilling an order for Saudi Arabia, which amounted to 247 tonnes of equipment worth £70,000, to be sent by train. It was part of a two-year contract to supply 1,100 oil engines for an irrigation scheme.

■ WORKMEN building the new sewerage system along Manthorpe Road to Marston in the 1930s.

■ AN engine driver at Harlaxton Quarry Cyril Marshall and some of his workmates from Stewart & Lloyds. His locomotive, pulling trucks of iron ore, had just run out of control between Hungerton and Swinehill, Harlaxton, in July 1951.

■ GRANTHAM Telephone Exchange at the Post Office, St Peter's Hill, in 1953. The 24 girls worked from 8am to 6pm, with 17 men taking over the night shift. Together they handled 5,000 calls a day, 2,000 of them local. At peak times they handled 500 calls an hour.

■ A WORKMAN at Vacu-lug, Gonerby Hill Foot, tidying up following a fire in 1954.

■ THE front offices being built for BMARCo, Springfield Road, in 1938. Many people will remember them as whitewashed.

■ WOMEN at BMARCo Springfield Road factory making shells in about 1962.

■ GRANTHAM Steam Laundry (later Fenland) on Belton Lane. It was pulled down for a housing development in the 1990s. The front boundary wall was retained.

■ THE scene in this picture looks almost Dickensian, yet it was taken less than 60 years ago. It is Grantham Steam Laundry in about 1950, and the rollers are giant mangles. Even in these conditions, however, the ladies do not appear to have the washday blues.

The building, on Belton Lane, opposite the Harrowby Lane junction, was built in about 1900. It later became Fenland Laundry and was pulled down in the 1980s for a housing development.

■ INSIDE TDG's empty warehouse, Trent Road, where it was about to store millions of tins of pet food in about 1989. It later became a B&Q distribution depot but closed in 2007.

■ THE same warehouse, only now full of pet food.

■ THE driver of this fork-lift truck at TDG's warehouse, Trent Road, misjudged the amount of space he had to manoeuvre in 1989.

■ CADDY Castings is one of the town's oldest manufacturing companies. It was formed in 1896 in Nottingham, and moved to the former brickworks in Springfield Road in the 1960s. It makes most types of casting, except steel. The picture shows Arthur Wheeler pouring the molten metal from a ladle into a mould in 1996.

■ THE site of the former BMARCo social club being used for breaking commercial vehicles in 1999.

■ AN aerial view of Aveling Barford's factory in Syston in 1952. This later became Barfords of Belton, and then Industrial Engines.

■ FOSTERS, the builders, are best known for the Manthorpe estate and smaller ones in the Harlaxton Road area. This is their joinery workshop on Wharf Road in about 1960. The company closed in the mid-1980s.

Focus on play

GRANTHAM was once voted the Most Boring Town in Britain but, as these pictures show, there has always been plenty to do.

■ *PUSS in Boots* was Ruston and Hornsby's pantomime in 1953, with Barrie Cox as Puss. The pantos were held in the works canteen until 1953, when it became the Coronation Hall, off Station Road East.

■ The Ruston & Hornsby Panto in 1952 was *Cinderella*. Buttons (Harold Woods) is pictured fitting the shoe on to Cinderella's (Ethel Richardson) foot. Others pictured are: Sylvia Crowson (Dandini), Barbara Gibson and Barbara Franks (pages), Queenie Ingram (Prince Charming), Fred Rounding (Baron Overdraft), Claude Hardy and Peter Foister (Ugly Sisters).

■ THE Vagabonds skiffle group including Roy Taylor (later Vince Eager) and Brian "Licorice" Locking who joined Cliff Richard's group The Shadows in the 1957 Ruston and Hornsby pantomime *Babes in the Wood*.

■ THE chorus line in the 1951 Ruston and Hornsby production of *Jack and the Beanstalk*.

■ THE Earl of Ancaster opened 2nd Grantham (St Wulfram's) Boy Scouts sixth annual garden fête in Church House grounds, Castlegate, in 1954. The fête raised £70 for scout funds.

■ THE beck which ran down the southern side of Dysart Park was always very popular with children. They used to drink from it, too, claiming the iron was good for them. The picture was taken in about 1937. The stream was variously known as Grantham Spa or Chalybeate Spring. These were also the days before the vandals paid attention to the pavilion that housed the bowls club and the park keeper's office.

■ THEY bred them tough in 1952, when indoor swimming pools were unheard of. Instead, even in May, hundreds would turn out at Wyndham Park to enjoy the great outdoors. Schoolchildren would go in when the water temperature wasn't much above 40 degrees – Fahrenheit that is, not Celcius! The grassy bank on the riverside was always an attraction, although the ground around sometimes got muddy, and most people at would at some point stub their toes on the concrete or plain wood steps.

Once the indoor pool opened, the days of the outdoor ones were numbered. Wyndham Park was first a skateboard rink, then home to Grantham Model Boat Club.

■ CHILDREN enjoy playing near the weir in the river in Wyndham Park in the 1950s, a practice no longer encouraged.

■ A YOUNG angler with his catch from the Witham in Wyndham Park in the 1950s.

■ THESE delighted schoolboys were among more than 6,000 spectators who turned out for Grantham FC's second preliminary FA Cup round in 1954 against Boston United. Boston were two goals up before the break but a gallant fight back saw two goals in as many minutes for Town.

■ WOOLSTHORPE-by-Belvoir was one of many villages to have a band. Others in the area included Bottesford and Barrowby. This picture shows Woolsthorpe founder member T.W. Worsdale retiring in 1962, and handing his baton to Norman Cook.

■ VOLUNTEERS helped out at the old London Road football ground in 1966, as concrete terracing replaced the hard ash on Spion Kop, a small hillock near the entrance.

■ GRANTHAM FC fans turning up for the FA Cup match at home to Altrincham in December 1967. They are going down the slope to the old London Road ground.

Across the road is motor dealership North Road Garages.

■ A TEAM struggles on the weir in the 1983 annual raft race on the River Witham from the Paddock to Wyndham Park.

■ ONE crew managed to take the Sedgwick Meadows weir in their stride.

■ PAMELA Keen, proprietor of Grantham School of Dance, Mount Street, Grantham, with some of the 250 children who attended in 1985. She had taken over from Gloria Hill six years previously.

■ THE modern façade of the £11,000 extension at BMARCo social club was one of the most attractive in the county. When this picture was taken in 1963, the Springfield Road venue was one of the most popular dance halls in town, with top groups and organist Ken Simmonds playing there on a regular basis.

■ BMARCo's Social Club, Springfield Road, being demolished in 1999. The club had been a mecca for local dance bands and rock groups but failed to stay afloat after the factory closed. Affordable homes were built on the site.

Focus on celebrities

JUST a few of the famous faces who have paid a visit to Grantham.

■ PRIME Minister Harold Macmillan with Lady Dorothy visiting Grantham (Westgate) during the 1959 General Election.

■ COMEDIAN Benny Hill (not Frankie Vaughan as stated in *Grantham in the News 1951-1975*) paid a visit in 1957, to open the High Street hairdressing salon run by the Misses Griffin.

■ STAN Laurel and Oliver Hardy came to town in 1952 to open the Trades Fair. They are pictured in Colin Tipler's outfitters shop, High Street, with their wives and Gladys Foster, who went on to become Mayor of Grantham.

■ TOP of the bill at the Granada cinema in 1960 was entertainer Max Bygraves. He is signing his autograph for manager 'Uncle' Harry Sanders.

■ NORTH Road Garages moved from Great Ponton, where it was formed in the 1920s, to the old brewery site, London Road, Grantham, in 1963. It was opened by World Motor Racing Champion Graham Hill, who drove for BRM.

■ ACTOR Sam Kydd was in town in September 1966 for Earlesfield Church carnival, which raised £350 towards the Church of the Epiphany building fund. Mr Kydd starred in popular TV show, *Orlando*, in which he played the title role. The series was a spin-off of *Crane*, starring Patrick Allen. He accepted the invitation to come to Grantham by Coun Fred Foster, with whom Mr Kydd was a prisoner of war in Poland. The carnival was held on the playground of St Hugh's School.

■ FAVOURITE Aussie Rolf Harris was at Belton House to open the new season in 1982.

■ ACTOR Geoffrey Hughes was at A.C. Williams' 25th anniversary in August 1982 when they sponsored the fête at Ancaster. About 4,000 people turned up. He was best known as Eddie Yates in *Coronation Street* and more recently as Onslow in *Keeping Up Appearances*. With him are Isobel Sutton and her son Nigel.

■ YES, that really is Hollywood superstar, George C. Scott! He was filming *The Last Days of General Patton*, for CBNS television, reprising his part from the 1970 film *Lust for Glory*. Harlaxton Manor was the setting for the Third Army HQ, Bavaria.

■ MARGARET Thatcher visited her old school, Kesteven and Grantham Girls' School, in 1977; one of several visits to the school where she was once joint head girl.

■ ACTRESS Judy Campbell (centre) was in town in 1996 to unveil a plaque at Iceland supermarket, St Peter's Hill, marking her father's role in the film industry. John Campbell owned three cinemas in the town.

Grantham-born Judy is pictured with two former Picture House employees, including Winifred Lawrence (right). Behind is a mock-up of the St Peter's Hill cinema.

With Miss Campbell was her daughter, actress Jane Birkin, not pictured.

■ *CORONATION Street* star Patricia Phoenix, who played Elsie Tanner, was in Foston in the late 1950s to open the village garden fête.

■ POPULAR TV series *Auf Weidersehen, Pet* was filmed in the area in 1985. The Geordie builders had moved from Dusseldorf to convert a manor house in the Midlands. Filming was at Denton, Car Colston and Bingham, but was mainly centred on the Peacock Inn, Redmile. Here, autograph hunters are distracted by Wayne (Gary Holton).

■ Gary Holton takes a break in the street at Redmile.

■ BARRY (Timothy Spall) signs an autograph for a young fan who already seems to be picking up a builder's bad habits.

■ A PARTING gesture to an unfriendly landlord, the lads brick up the doorway when they leave.

■ LED by Bomber (Pat Roach) are most of the principal cast: Wayne (Gary Holton), Barry (Timothy Spall), Moxey (Chris Fairbank), Dennis (Tim Healy) and Oz (Jimmy Nail).

■ THE actors including Pat Roach, Jimmy Nail and Tim Healy take a break as a pony and trap goes past in rural Redmile.

Focus on festivals

THERE is nothing new about parades through the town. They originated with the military, but civilians with floats began the annual events in the 19th century, with parades of horses and decorated cycles. During the 1920s and 1930s, the annual 'Rag' raised funds for the hospital. In the 1960s, Aveling Barford introduced their annual gala, and when the company could endure no more losses, a committee spearheaded by Roy Wright continued the good work with the Grantham Carnival from the mid-1980s.

■ ASDA won the commercial section for the best float in the 2001 Grantham Carnival parade with its vision of shopping in the next millennium.

■ GRANTHAM students taking part in what was then their annual rag week in October 1969. Events included kidnapping the town's Tory MP Joe Godber, although the stunt only managed to raise £7.55 ransom! This was one of only four floats that year, with Kesteven and Grantham Girls' School depicting the Isle of Wight Folk Festival.

■ GRANTHAM College students won first prize for the float 'sleep in' during the 1969 rag week. They are pictured in Huntingtower Road.

■ THE 1976 Barford's Gala where Kesteven Rugby Club present Fred Flintstone and friends.

■ THE Aveling Barford gala parade makes its way along High Street in 1976.

■ AN Aveling Barford road roller conveys the Carnival Princess in 1982.

■ WALTON Girls School's float in the 1987 Grantham Carnival on Bridge End Road.

■ A LONDON bus, with Cheryl Baker of TV's *Record Breakers* on the top deck, attracts the interest of a cameraman in the 1987 Grantham Carnival. Miss Baker was there to oversee an attempt at a world record conga.

■ GRANTHAM Young Farmers' float.

■ EARLESFIELD Tenants and Residents Association float.

■ HARRISON House float's in the 1988 Grantham Carnival.

■ GRANTHAM Young Farmers float.

■ THE Woodland Trust float.

■ AN AVELING Barford RD350 dump truck in the 1988 Grantham Carnival, passing the Phoenix Club on Bridge End Road.

■ THE Grantham Rag was a fund-raiser for Grantham Hospital in the early part of the 20th century. These pictures were taken in September 1929. Here, a float passes along North Street.

■ FIRST Aid men cross Avenue Road Bridge.

■ PEARSON'S Haulage in North Street.

■ THE Grantham Co-op's float in the big parade.

■ RUSTON and Hornsby Fire Brigade pass the corner of Grove End Road.

■ A CATTLE remover's lorry carrying Grantham Hospital's float along Avenue Road passes Welham Street.

■ GRANTHAM Borough Fire Brigade goes along North Street.

Focus on education

SCHOOLS and colleges in the Grantham area over the last century.

■ PUPILS at the Girls Central School in 1948. The school was then off Castlegate (down a footpath opposite Finkin Street). This later became the teaching centre, and then a nursery for Grantham College. In the centre of the picture is Miss Nina Hewitt, who had recently taken over from the school's first headteacher, Miss Jabbet. Miss Hewitt was still in charge when the school moved to Kitty Briggs Lane to become Walton Girls School in the late 1960s.

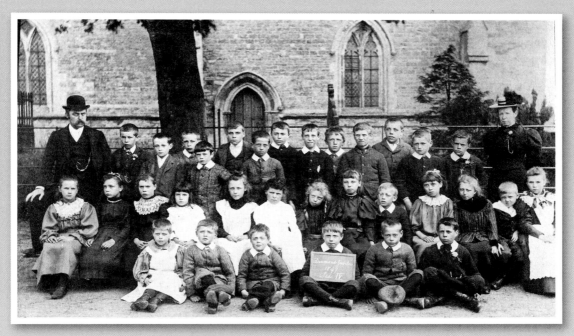

■ THIS picture was taken in 1897, to celebrate Queen Victoria's 60th year on the throne. They are the senior class of Great Gonerby School outside St Sebastian's Church.

■ TUCKED away surrounded by houses, a cinema and John Lee's rag and skin factory, Welby Street School was open for about 80 years. It closed in 1940 when pupil numbers had fallen so low that it was considered too expensive to run. The boys in this 1931 photograph look quaint now, in their short trousers and hobnail boots. Their clothes also confirm that the area was not a wealthy one.

The foundation stone of the school was incorporated in the Isaac Newton Centre. It was demolished in 1983 as Welby Street and Stanton Street fell to the developers.

■ THESE youngsters went to Woolsthorpe School in about 1947. Headteacher Mr T. Emmerton is on the left and his assistant, Mr Wakeley to the right. The children, from back left, are: Pat Williams, Roger Braisby, Jim Bullimore, Roger Pacey, Stan Bonshor, Dennis Braisby, Neville Smith, Vic Burgess and Horace Taylor. Middle: Ann Taylor, Mary Robinson, Sylvia Worsdale, Ella Burgess, Faith Finn, Sheila Pacey and Barbara Bonshor. Front: Helen Green, Pat Locke, Lavinia Morris, Wendy Barber, Barbara Stubley, and Rosamund Welbourn.

■ FRED Bennett, captain of the Boys' Central School's Smith House, receives the inter-house swimming trophy, the Samuel Thorp Memorial Shield, in 1954. Mr Thorp was the school's founding headteacher. The shield was presented by the Mayor of Grantham, Ernest Hardy.

■ THESE children were at Hough-on-the-Hill School in about 1956. The teachers are Mrs Gwyther (left) and Mrs Padgett. Like so many village schools in the Grantham area, it closed in the mid-1980s.

■ NATURALIST Peter Scott with principal Fred Johnson opening Grantham College of Further Education's new main building in September 1959.

■ PRINCIPAL of the Grantham College of Further Education, Fred Johnson (left), and county architect J.W.H. Barnes, study a model of the proposed main building in November 1954.

■ THE National School, Castlegate, may have been built in 1859, but don't tell its pupils the buildings are past it. The *Journal* described the buildings as 'decaying' in 1996 and was swamped with letters from angry children. The article followed plans to build a new school next to Little Gonerby Infants, Sandon Road, falling through.

■ THE National School took the plunge by installing a gas-heated swimming pool, 33ft by 25ft, in 1969. It cost £2,000.

■ THE 26 infants at Folkingham School were excited when a mobile classroom was delivered in 1971, to give them more space. They had been cramped in one small room while the juniors had the larger room. The new 32ft by 18ft classroom delighted staff and pupils alike.

■ YOUNG ladies at Sir William Robertson School, Welbourn, prepare for a fashion show in 1971.

■ COLSTERWORTH School in 1975, where pupils were enjoying a Dutch week. They learned about Holland together with the song *Tulips from Amsterdam*.

■ MAYPOLE dancing was among the attractions at the Blessed Hugh More School's annual fête in July 1981. It was opened by the Royal Assocation of Disability and Rehabilitation Man of the Year, Sqdn Ldr Gerard Margiotta, of Grantham.

■ LONG before Victoria Wood made *Dinnerladies* famous, they were an active force in Grantham. At one time, nearly every school ensured its children had a hot meal every day. By the time this picture was taken, in the late 1960s, lumpy custard and watery cabbage had been all but eliminated. These are the dinner ladies at St Anne's School, Harrowby Road, in their new kitchen.

■ THE 74 pupils at Ancaster were getting excited in 1985, as they were having a new school in the village. They were saying goodbye to the old one built in 1862.

■ LITTLE Gonerby School, built at the junction of New Street and Brownlow Street in 1863, moved to bigger and brighter premises. The children took over the former Boys' Central School, Sandon Road, in 1985, after the Central moved to Rushcliffe Road. This wasn't their first move either. For the first 12 years the children had been taught in a room in Union Street. The old school became a residential home.

■ THE new Little Gonerby School in 1985.

■ MUSIC-MAKING pupils at the Isaac Newton School in 1985.

■ KESTEVEN and Grantham Girls' School used their brand new hall for the first time in February 1986. The hall completed a number of additions to the school, including a new block with seven laboratories, four practical rooms and a classroom. The main school was also upgraded. The picture shows headteacher Margaret Wilson addressing the pupils. It was opened later in the year by Prime Minister Margaret Thatcher, an old girl of the school.

Focus from the air

ONE of the most fascinating ways of viewing any town is to see it from a different angle. Even those who are seasoned fliers seldom see Grantham from the air.

■ GRANTHAM looking from the south, showing a pronounced curve in the railway line on the left. The buildings bottom left are on South Parade retail park. Just above them are Curry's and B&Q, while some of the old Ruston and Hornsby buildings still survive behind them. The large white-roofed building in the centre is Safeway supermarket. In the top left are the derelict Corus buildings which ran alongside Dysart Road. The photograph was taken in 2001.

■ THIS photograph was taken by the Royal Flying Corps in 1918. The road in the centre is Elmer Street, with High Street to the left and Castlegate to the right. In High Street, about halfway up, it shows clearly the old National Provincial Bank (later Newton Fallowell estate agents) jutting into the road.

■ LOOKING west from St Wulfram's Church in 1952, this picture shows a lot of buildings that are no longer there, especially at the bottom of Watergate and North Street.

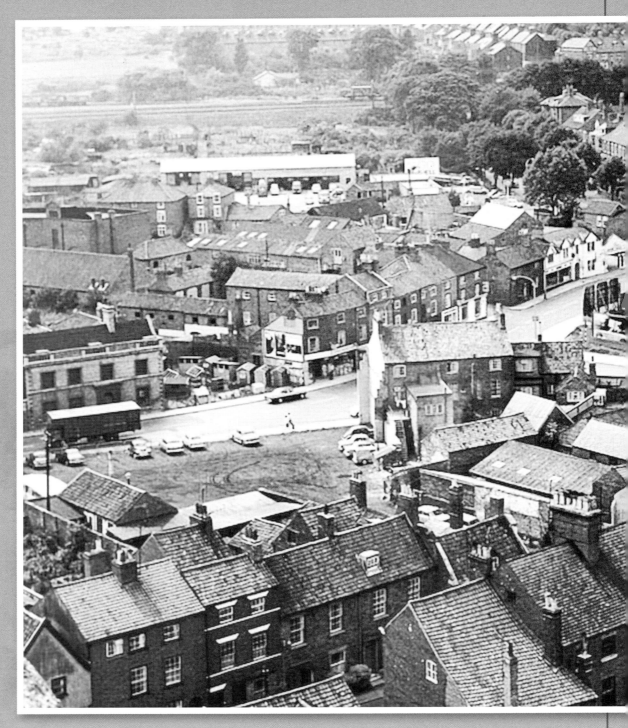

■ THE view from St Wulfram's looking to the north-west. On the centre left is Watergate car park with Swinegate at the bottom. The cleared ground, centre right, shows the James Street–Vere Street crossroads. It was developed as Premier Court.

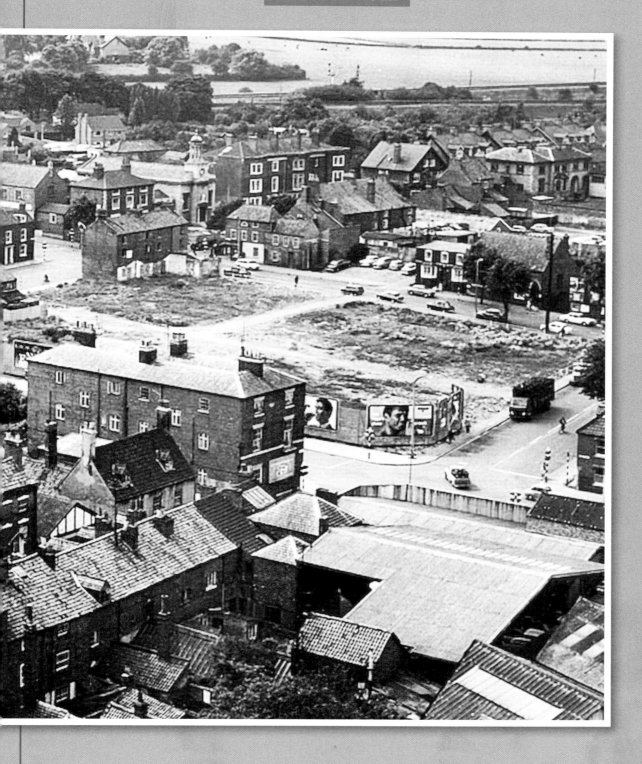

■ THE east side of Grantham has changed a lot since this picture was taken from St Wulfram's Church in about 1970. The College has been developed extensively, while Pidcock's Welham Street maltings (top right) were about to be demolished together with the houses in Agnes Street, Agnes Terrace and Witham Terrace.